*I love it when you laugh.*
*I pray that God fills our*
*marriage with even more of*
*that wonderful sound.*

**A joyful heart is good medicine.**
PROVERBS 17:22 NASB

**Laughter is the most beautiful**
**and bene...**
**God ever g...**

*Chu...*

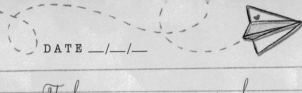

DATE __/__/__

*I know you can make an awesome difference in people's lives. I'm already thanking God for how He will use you even more than He already has.*

**May the favor of the Lord
our God rest on us;
establish the work of our hands
for us—yes, establish the
work of our hands.**
PSALM 90:17 NIV

You are never too old to set
another goal or to dream a new dream.
C. S. LEWIS

I asked God
to help you feel
soooo loved.

Has He answered
my prayer yet?

I found the one my heart loves.
SONG OF SONGS 3:4 NIV

Nothing can bring a real
sense of security into the home
except true love.

Billy Graham

*I thank God that He gave me somebody who understands me.
Nobody gets me like you do.
I want to thank you too.*

You husbands in the same way,
live with your wives in an understanding way.

I PETER 3:7 NASB

To be fully known and truly loved is, well,
a lot like being loved by God. It is what we
need more than anything. It liberates
us from pretense, humbles us out of our
self-righteousness, and fortifies us for any
difficulty life can throw at us.

*Timothy Keller*

DATE __/__/__

*I know God has the power to make us fall in love all over again. Every. Single. Day. Let's both ask Him to do just that!*

**God is love. Whoever lives in love lives in God, and God in them.**
I JOHN 4:16 NIV

**When we show love to others, God's presence is with us.**

*Linda Evans Shepherd*

*When I think it's not possible for you to make me any happier, you do. Thanking God right now!*

You will show me the way of life.
Being with You is to be full of joy.
In Your right hand
there is happiness forever.

PSALM 16:11 NLV

To love someone means
to see them as God intended them.

*Fyodor Dostoevsky*

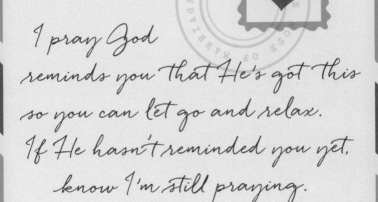

DATE __/__/__

I pray God
reminds you that He's got this
so you can let go and relax.
If He hasn't reminded you yet,
know I'm still praying.

"Do not fear, for I am with you.
Do not be afraid, for I am your God.
I will give you strength, and for sure
I will help you. Yes, I will hold you up
with My right hand that is right and good."
ISAIAH 41:10 NLV

Be assured, if you walk with Him
and look to Him and expect help
from Him, He will never fail you.

George Mueller

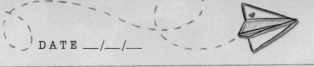

*I adore you. And I told God that today when I thanked Him for you. Thought I would remind you too.*

**You are a garden spring,
a well of fresh water,
and streams flowing from Lebanon.**
SONG OF SOLOMON 4:15 NASB

Love like there's no tomorrow,
and if tomorrow comes, love again.
MAX LUCADO

*You can have my everything. It's yours. God said so. Praying I model this move.*

The wife is not the boss of her own body. It belongs to the husband. And in the same way, the husband is not the boss of his own body. It belongs to the wife.

I CORINTHIANS 7:4 NLV

O divine Master, grant that I might not so much seek... to be loved as to love.

*St. Francis of Assisi*

DATE __/__/__

*I am praying This
for you: XOXOXOXOXO.
I Think you know what
    I mean. Sending love
and warmth your way!*

We don't know what God wants us
to pray for. But the Holy Spirit
prays for us with groanings
that cannot be expressed in words.

ROMANS 8:26 NLT

Love is like the wind; you can't
see it but you can feel it.

*Nicholas Sparks*

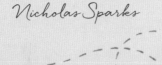

DATE __/__/__

Love does kind things like rubbing necks or feet when the one we love is tense. I thank God that you are so kind and so generous with your massages. Massage? Now? Yes, please.

**Love is kind.**
I CORINTHIANS 13:4 NIV

Great marriages are made when husbands and wives make a lot of everyday choices that say "I love you," rather than choices that say "I love me."

*Matthew Jacobson*

XOXOXOXOXOXOXOXOXO

DATE __/__/__

Love tears up any mental list of past hurts and tosses it where it belongs.
As I prayed, I tossed those old hurts into the hands of our loving Savior.

**[Love] keeps no record of wrongs.**
I CORINTHIANS 13:5 NIV

**A happy marriage is the union of two good forgivers.**
*Ruth Bell Graham*

DATE ___/___/___

*Your future is bright,
and I ask God to help
you remember that.
I'll help you remember too.*

"For I know the plans I have for you,"
says the LORD. "They are plans
for good and not for disaster,
to give you a future and a hope."

JEREMIAH 29:11 NLT

Within this Christian vision of marriage,
here's what it means to fall in love. It is to look
at another person and get a glimpse of what God
is creating and say, "I see who God is making
you, and it excites me! I want to be part of that."

*Timothy Keller*

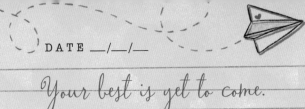

Your best is yet to come. Cliché? Maybe. True. Totally. God hinted that you might need to hear that today. I'm praying that you believe it for yourself as strongly as I believe it for you.

**Now to Him who is able to do far more abundantly beyond all that we ask or think, according to the power that works within us, to Him be the glory.**

EPHESIANS 3:20-21 NASB

Never be afraid to trust an unknown future to a known God.

CORRIE TEN BOOM

*I pray for your health and for you to feel good physically, mentally, emotionally, and spiritually. I can't imagine a day without you.*

I hope all is well with you
and that you are as healthy
in body as you are strong in spirit.

III JOHN 1:2 NLT

Pay mind to your own life,
your own health, and wholeness.

*Frederick Buechner*

DATE __/__/__

*Remember those sparks
we felt when dating?
Buckle up, baby, because
I'm praying that
God reignites them.*

Come, let's drink deeply of love till morning;
let's enjoy ourselves with love!
PROVERBS 7:18 NIV

The word "romance," according
to the dictionary, means excitement,
adventure, and something extremely real.
Romance should last a lifetime.

*Billy Graham*

DATE __/__/__

I've noticed the times you've put me before yourself and others. I see. God sees. May you know His "well done."

**[Love] isn't always "me first."**
I CORINTHIANS 13:5 THE MESSAGE

**You can give without loving,
but you can never love without giving.**

*Victor Hugo*

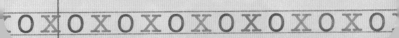

DATE __/__/__

*I asked God to direct your dreams toward Him in order to discover His path to your greatest success. I can't wait to see what He's going to do through you.*

**Take delight in the LORD,
and He will give you the desires of your heart.**
PSALM 37:4 NIV

**Jesus gives us hope because
He keeps us company, has a vision,
and knows the way we should go.**

*Max Lucado*

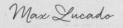

I hope you never get tired of hearing how much I love you. Because I never get tired of saying it—both to you and to God when I pray for you. I told Him again today.

How beautiful and how delightful you are,
My love, with all your charms!
SONG OF SOLOMON 7:6 NASB

In the Lord's plans for the world there is no work more important than the work of relationship, and no relationship is more important than that of one's marriage.

*Mike Mason*

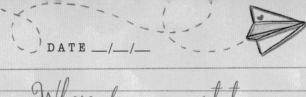

Where do you want to go
this weekend? I asked God
to put the perfect place
in your mind. I trust that
He did. Let's go have some fun.

Come, my beloved,
let us go out into the country,
let us spend the night in the villages.
SONG OF SOLOMON 7:11 NASB

When God brought the first man
his spouse, He brought him
not just a lover but the friend
his heart had been seeking.
TIMOTHY KELLER

I know you hate it when your favorite team loses. So I asked God to help you keep it in perspective and to show me how I can help lift your spirits. Hug it out?

A time to cry and a time to laugh.
A time to grieve and a time to dance.

ECCLESIASTES 3:4 NLT

One day someone is going
to hug you so tight that all your
broken pieces fit back together.

*Anonymous*

I pray that God revives and restores the "first love" feels we had when we got married. So brace yourself for butterfly overload.

Sustain me with raisin cakes,
refresh me with apples,
because I am lovesick.
SONG OF SOLOMON 2:5 NASB

A successful marriage requires
falling in love many times,
always with the same person.

*Mignon McLaughlin*

*I asked God to remind us that nothing is too difficult for Him to handle. So let's catch a wave knowing He's in control.*

This hope is a strong and trustworthy anchor for our souls. It leads us through the curtain into God's inner sanctuary.

HEBREWS 6:19 NLT

Hope is called the anchor of the soul...because it gives stability to the Christian life. But hope is not simply a "wish" (I wish that such-and-such would take place); rather, it is that which latches on to the certainty of the promises of the future that God has made.

*R. C. Sproul*

XOXOXOXOXOXOXOXOXOXO

DATE __/__/__

*I just want you to know
I'm here. I'm willing
and ready to truly listen
when you're ready to talk.*

My dear brothers and sisters,
take note of this: Everyone should be
quick to listen, slow to speak
and slow to become angry.

JAMES 1:19 NIV

Listening is where love begins.

*Fred Rogers*

*I miss you when you're away.*
*And I pray that God*
*brings me to your mind*
*with a very special thought.*
*You know the thought*
*I had in mind?*

**Let his left hand be under my head**
**and his right hand embrace me.**
SONG OF SOLOMON 8:3 NASB

**Their lips brushed like young**
**wildflowers in the wind.**

*F. Scott Fitzgerald*

*I ask God to remind us both
that He is the Source
of all we need. We can breathe
easy, knowing He'll provide.*

**God will generously provide all
you need. Then you will always
have everything you need and plenty
left over to share with others.**

II CORINTHIANS 9:8 NLT

God's work done in God's way
will never lack God's supply.
HUDSON TAYLOR

I thanked God for you today as I was praying, and it made my heart smile. I hope knowing I'm thankful for you makes your heart smile too.

I thank my God in all my remembrance of you, always offering prayer with joy in my every prayer for you all.

PHILIPPIANS 1:3-4 NASB

One smile can't change the world, but your smile changes mine.

Zakiya and Majidmajid

DATE __/__/__

I ask God to help both
of us give each other
the benefit of the doubt when
we misunderstand each other.
After all, we're on the same
side. And a dash of grace
can go a long way.

If it is possible, as far as it depends on you,
live at peace with everyone.

ROMANS 12:18 NIV

When you forgive, you love. And when
you love, God's light shines upon you.

Jon Krakauer

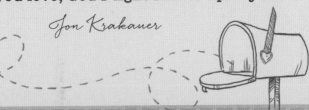

*I love it when people notice the authenticity of our love and say that it encourages them. I pray God will use us to build up other couples.*

Let your light shine before men in such a way that they may see your good works, and glorify your Father who is in heaven.

MATTHEW 5:16 NASB

Don't shine so that others will see you. Shine so that through you, others will see Him.

*Unknown*

XOXOXOXOXOXOXOXOXOXO

DATE ___/___/___

*I asked God to shower you with His blessings and favor today. The umbrella is by the front door. You're going to need it.*

I will make them and the places surrounding my hill a blessing. I will send down showers in season; there will be showers of blessing.

EZEKIEL 34:26 NIV

However many blessings we expect from God, His infinite liberality will always exceed all our wishes and our thoughts.

*John Calvin*

DATE __/__/__

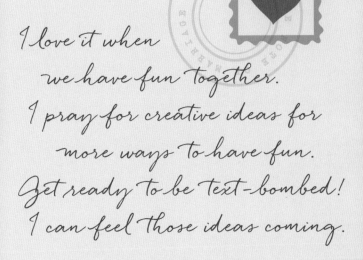

I love it when
we have fun together.
I pray for creative ideas for
more ways to have fun.
Get ready to be text-bombed!
I can feel those ideas coming.

There, in the presence of the LORD
your God, you and your families shall
eat and shall rejoice in everything
you have put your hand to, because
the LORD your God has blessed you.

DEUTERONOMY 12:7 NIV

It is not how much we have, but how
much we enjoy, that makes happiness.

*Charles Spurgeon*

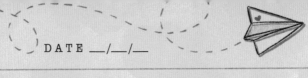

DATE __/__/__

I want to fix it and make
everything better for you.
I really do. But I can't.
So I'm asking the One who can.
He is able. In the meantime,
how about a hug?

**Cast all your anxiety on Him
because He cares for you.**

I PETER 5:7 NIV

God is looking for those with
whom He can do the impossible.
What a pity that we plan only
the things we can do by ourselves!

A. W. TOZER

*I love that your eyes light up when I walk into the room. I pray that God will make it happen a lot.*

With joy you will draw water
from the wells of salvation.
ISAIAH 12:3 NIV

God made human beings as He made
His other creatures, to be happy.

*Charles Spurgeon*

DaySpring

I ask God to mold me
into the kind of life
partner you need most.
I want to be that person
for you—and God can
make it happen.
Tell me if it's working.

In your relationships with one another,
have the same mindset as Christ Jesus.

PHILIPPIANS 2:5 NIV

He said, "Love...as I have loved you."
We cannot love too much.

*Amy Carmichael*

DATE __/__/__

*I accept you
exactly how you are. Every strength.
Every weakness. Everything that
makes you, you.*

You were bought at a price.
Therefore honor God with your bodies.

I CORINTHIANS 6:20 NIV

I look at you, and I see the rest
of my life in front of my eyes.

*Anonymous*

XOXOXOXOXOXOXOXOXO

DATE __/__/__

*In my prayer today I said
to God with much gratitude,
"Well done!" He did a great
thing in bringing us together.*

Flowers appear on the earth;
the season of singing has come,
the cooing of doves is heard in our land.
SONG OF SONGS 2:12 NIV

The first step to finding a God-written
love story is handing the pen
to the true Author of romance.

*Leslie Ludy*

I asked God to help
us plan wisely for our future.
He told me to just push
the "easy button" and let
Him take it from here.

**Commit to the LORD whatever you do,
and He will establish your plans.**
PROVERBS 16:3 NIV

**Faith makes all things possible.
Love makes all things easy.**
Dwight L. Moody

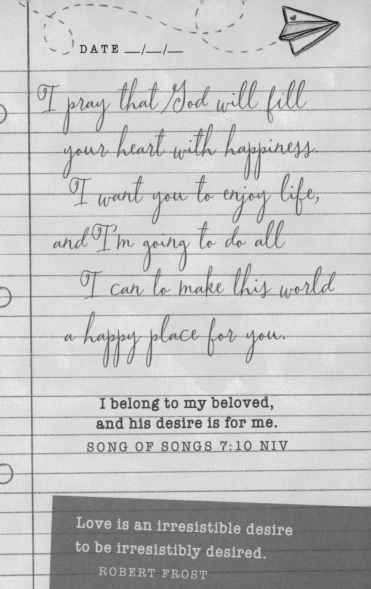

DATE __/__/__

*I pray that God will fill your heart with happiness. I want you to enjoy life, and I'm going to do all I can to make this world a happy place for you.*

**I belong to my beloved, and his desire is for me.**
SONG OF SONGS 7:10 NIV

Love is an irresistible desire
to be irresistibly desired.
ROBERT FROST

*Today I invited God to show up in our marriage in a way that makes us both say "Wow!" Ready for some wishes to come true?*

**May He grant you your heart's desire.**

PSALM 20:4 NASB

**When you love someone, all your saved-up wishes start coming out.**

*Elizabeth Bowen*

*Love never stops.*
*So I'm praying that you*
*remember how much*
*I love you. And how long*
*I will love you: forever.*

**Love keeps going to the end.**
I CORINTHIANS 13:7 THE MESSAGE

**I will spend an eternity loving you,**
**caring for you, respecting you,**
**showing you every day that I hold**
**you as high as the stars.**

*Steve Maraboli*

DATE __/__/__

*I pray that God blesses our marriage with mutual love and respect.*

Here is a simple, rule-of-thumb guide for behavior: Ask yourself what you want people to do for you, then grab the initiative and do it for them. Add up God's Law and Prophets and this is what you get.

MATTHEW 7:12 THE MESSAGE

The foundation of a marriage can be narrowed down to two simple words: love and respect.

*Tony Evans*

OXOXOXOXOXOXOXOXOXO

DATE __/__/__

*I pray that we have more moments when we can just lay side by side and forget the world. I want to snuggle with you all-day-long.*

Then God blessed the seventh day and made it holy, because on it He rested from all the work of creating that He had done.

GENESIS 2:3 NIV

Two hearts in love need no words.

*Marceline Desbordes-Valmore*

That last scoop of ice cream belongs to you. I pray God will help you see how much I love you in my actions. (Better hurry up and eat it, though!)

"We are more happy when
we give than when we receive."
ACTS 20:35 NLV

Love is when the other person's happiness
is more important than your own.

H. Jackson Brown Jr.

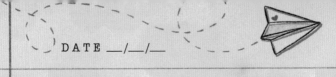

DATE __/__/__

*I asked God to stoke the flame of passion and romance in our marriage.*

*XOXO*

Put me over your heart and on your arm,
never to be taken off.
For love is as strong as death.
Jealousy is as hard as the grave.
Its bright light is like the light of fire,
the very fire of the Lord.

SONG OF SOLOMON 8:6 NLV

We go together like campfires
and marshmallows.

ANONYMOUS

I pray for our marriage and ask God to help us continue growing as a couple. And I can't wait to see how He answers that prayer.

May the Lord cause you to increase and abound in love for one another.

I THESSALONIANS 3:12 NASB

Marriage is a mosaic you build with your spouse—millions of tiny moments that create your love story.

*Jennifer Smith*

*I ask God to help you understand and embrace this Truth: I am more me when I'm with you. Thank you for helping me be the best version of me.*

**I always thank my God for you and for the gracious gifts He has given you.**

I CORINTHIANS 1:4 NLT

**Love is a partnership of two unique people who bring out the very best in each other and who know that even though they are wonderful as individuals, they are even better together.**

*Barbara Cage*

*I pray that God shows
you all the greatness
He—and I—see in you.
I want you to see it too.*

**[Love] always looks for the best.**
I CORINTHIANS 13:7 THE MESSAGE

**All of us have special ones
who have loved us into being.**

*Fred Rogers*

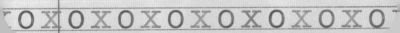

DaySpring

*Love waits well.*
*So I'm praying we*
*can be more patient*
*with each other.*

**Love is patient.**
I CORINTHIANS 13:4 NIV

**Come and sit and ask Him**
**whatever is on your heart....**
**He has all the time in the world.**
*Max Lucado*

DATE __/__/__

*I ask God to*
*bless you with His favor,*
*calm you with His peace,*
*and be kind to you,*
*today and every day.*

"May the Lord bring good to you
and keep you. May the Lord make His
face shine upon you, and be kind to you.
May the Lord show favor toward you,
and give you peace."

NUMBERS 6:24-26 NLV

To love is to compassionately
and righteously pursue
the well-being of another.

*Tony Evans*

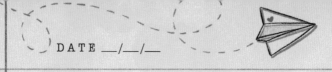

DATE __/__/__

*I pray that God
gives us His eyes...
His heart...His grace...
and His love for each other.*

**Beloved, let us love one another,
for love is from God; and everyone who
loves is born of God and knows God.**

I JOHN 4:7 NASB

We come to love not by finding
a perfect person, but by learning
to see an imperfect person perfectly.

SAM KEEN

I tell people often how much I admire you. I told God today that I'm your number one fan. He said we'll have to share that role. We love loving you!

Now faith, hope, love, abide these three; but the greatest of these is love.

I CORINTHIANS 13:13 NASB

The greatest marriages are built on teamwork, a mutual respect, a healthy dose of admiration, and a never-ending portion of love and grace.

Fawn Weaver

*I pray that God gives us imaginative ways to express our love for each other. Let's make an "express-our-love" to-do list. (I know what's #1.)*

**May he kiss me with
the kisses of his mouth!
For your love is better than wine.**
SONG OF SOLOMON 1:2 NASB

**Marriage is a commitment—a decision
to do, all through life, that which
will express love for one's spouse.**

*Herman H. Kieval*

DATE __/__/__

I asked God
to make our marriage magical.
(Cue the shooting stars.)

Ah Lord God! Behold, You have made
the heavens and the earth by Your
great power and by Your outstretched
arm! Nothing is too difficult for You.
JEREMIAH 32:17 NASB

Where there is great love,
there are always miracles.

Willa Cather

XOXOXOXOXOXOXOXOXO

DATE __/__/__

*I pray that God helps us savor the sweet smiles and stolen glances despite the busyness of life.*

You have made my heart beat faster,
my sister, my bride;
You have made my heart beat faster
with a single glance of your eyes.
SONG OF SOLOMON 4:9 NASB

Let us always meet each other
with a smile, for the smile
is the beginning of love.
*Mother Teresa*

*I pray that love
is always the heartbeat
of our home.*

**Love never fails.**
I CORINTHIANS 13:8 NASB

**The best thing to hold
onto in life is each other.**

*Audrey Hepburn*

I admire your courage,
and I know sometimes life
is really hard. That's why
I ask God to give you more
courage and His strength.

**[Love] always protects.**
I CORINTHIANS 13:7 NIV

Let encouragement be a way
of life in your marriage and you
will develop a connection that goes
beyond the "everyday-ness" of life.
BRUCE WILKINSON AND HEATHER HAIR

*I ask God to show us how we are to take over the planet for His glory.*

Let us not lose heart in doing good,
for in due time we will reap
if we do not grow weary.

GALATIANS 6:9 NASB

Love does not consist in gazing at
each other, but in looking outward
together in the same direction.

*Antoine de Saint-Exupéry*

*I pray that we never
sacrifice the ultimate
for the urgent.
So I ask for greater
margin in our marriage.
For space to simply be.*

**"Be still, and know that I am God."**
PSALM 46:10 NIV

The more time you invest in a marriage,
the more valuable it becomes.

*Amy Grant*

DATE __/__/__

You have a true friend for life in me. God nudged me to remind you of that while I was praying for you. And you can trust me to keep praying.

**[Love] always trusts.**
I CORINTHIANS 13:7 NIV

Rest assured, the same One who holds the stars and planets in space, parted the Red Sea, and fed the 5,000 can take care of you.

*Edie Emory*

XOXOXOXOXOXOXOXOXOXO

*You are my wish come true.*
*I never want to live*
*a day without you.*

O my dove, in the clefts of the rock,
in the secret place of the steep pathway,
let me see your form,
let me hear your voice;
for your voice is sweet,
and your form is lovely.

SONG OF SOLOMON 2:14 NASB

I would rather share one lifetime with you
than face all the ages of this world alone.

*J. R. R. Tolkien*

*I asked God
To help us rekindle our
romance—and I saw
Him grab a match.*

May your fountain be blessed,
and may you rejoice
in the wife of your youth.
PROVERBS 5:18 NIV

God, in His genius and creativity,
designed us to both need Him
and to need each other.

*Susan Goss*

DaySpring

Toothpaste tubes squeezed in the middle? Toilet paper over or under? Seat up or seat down? Small things, but they matter. The big things matter too. I pray that God will help us honor each other's preferences in both the big and the little things.

**Love...doesn't force itself on others.**

I CORINTHIANS 13:5 THE MESSAGE

A marriage, of all places, should be highlighted with hearts of honor.

HEATHER HAIR

*I pray that God helps you fully feel my love. And I take requests!*

Do everything in love.

I CORINTHIANS 16:14 NIV

Love is always bestowed as a gift—
freely, willingly, and without
expectation. We don't love
to be loved; we love to love.

*Leo Buscaglia*

Want to show off God's love together? I asked Him to fill us up with so much love that it overflows onto others.

No one has ever seen God;
but if we love one another, God lives in us
and His love is made complete in us.

I JOHN 4:12 NIV

The measure of love is to
love without measure.

*St. Francis de Sales*

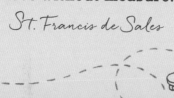

*I told on you to God today. I told Him you deserve a hundred kisses. Get ready!*

May my beloved come into his garden
and eat its choice fruits!

SONG OF SOLOMON 4:16 NASB

Relationships are like dances in which
people try to find whatever happens
to be the mutual rhythm in their lives.

*Fred Rogers*

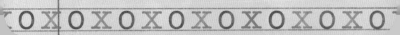

DATE __/__/__

Life happens. Bills need to be paid.
Dishes need to be washed.
Messy hair greets us in the morning.
But in the midst of it all, you are
still my fairy-tale happy ending.

**My beloved is mine, and I am his.**
SONG OF SOLOMON 2:16 NASB

**Grow old along with me!**
**The best is yet to be.**
*Robert Browning*

DATE __/__/__

*I ask God to help
us to love more freely,
kiss more frequently,
and pray more fervently.
When do you want to start?*

The fruit that comes from having
the Holy Spirit in our lives is: love,
joy, peace, not giving up, being kind,
being good, having faith.

GALATIANS 5:22 NLV

At the touch of love,
everyone becomes a poet.

*Plato*

*I pray that God fills our minds with positive thoughts about the present and affirming thoughts about our future.*

Whatever is true, whatever is honorable, whatever is right, whatever is pure, whatever is lovely, whatever is of good repute, if there is any excellence and if anything worthy of praise, dwell on these things.

PHILIPPIANS 4:8 NASB

The strongest and sweetest songs yet remain to be sung.

WALT WHITMAN

DATE __/__/__

I pray that God would give us a greater understanding of each other from which a deeper compassion can grow.

So, as those who have been chosen of God, holy and beloved, put on a heart of compassion, kindness, humility, gentleness and patience.

COLOSSIANS 3:12 NASB

If God's people are to be living examples of one thing, that thing ought to be—it must be—compassion.

*Chuck Swindoll*

Sometimes when things get tough or busy, I know you might feel alone. But I pray God reminds you that you're not alone. He is with you and for you. I am too.

**The LORD your God is with you wherever you go.**

JOSHUA 1:9 NASB

**Love is composed of a single soul inhabiting two bodies.**

*Aristotle*

*I hope you know
how truly special you are.
I ask God to remind
you of that truth.*

I will give thanks to You, for I am fearfully
and wonderfully made;
wonderful are Your works,
and my soul knows it very well.

PSALM 139:14 NASB

You've made this day a special day,
by just your being you.

*Fred Rogers*

DATE __/__/__

*I pray that God calms our emotions when we disagree so that we can grow in our love for each other and choose to focus on what really matters. And I have faith that God will do exactly that.*

**[Love] doesn't fly off the handle.**
I CORINTHIANS 13:5 THE MESSAGE

Young love is a flame; very pretty, often very hot and fierce, but still only light and flickering. The love of the older and disciplined heart is as coals, deep-burning, unquenchable.

*Henry Ward Beecher*

DATE __/__/__

*I pray God assures
you that He is with you
and that He is in your corner.
Every moment. Every day.
I am too.*

The LORD is near to all who call upon Him,
to all who call upon Him in truth.
He will fulfill the desire of those who fear Him;
He will also hear their cry
and will save them.

PSALM 145:18-19 NASB

My heart is, and always will be, yours.

*Jane Austen*

I ask God to let you know
just how attracted I am to you.
(Maybe He's already answered
that prayer and that's why
you're grinning so big!)

"How beautiful you are, my darling,
how beautiful you are!
Your eyes are like doves."
"How handsome you are, my beloved,
and so pleasant!
Indeed, our couch is luxuriant!"
SONG OF SOLOMON 1:15-16 NASB

Lovers alone wear sunlight.
E. E. CUMMINGS

I love our late-night runs to curb the munchies. I thank God for the simple things that make our marriage so sweet.

A loving doe, a graceful deer...
may you ever be intoxicated with her love.

PROVERBS 5:19 NIV

Every positive thing you do in
your relationship is foreplay.

*John Gottman*

DATE __/__/__

*I love how we help each other pursue God's purpose more intentionally than we ever did when we were on our own. I'm asking God to show us more of what we can do for Him as individuals and together.*

We are God's masterpiece. He has created us anew in Christ Jesus, so we can do the good things He planned for us long ago.

EPHESIANS 2:10 NLT

Marriage is a covenantal union designed to strengthen the capability of each partner to carry out the plan of God in their lives.

*Tony Evans*

*I thank God for sending me you. I know what love is because of you.*

**Always be humble and gentle.
Be patient with each other,
making allowance for each other's
faults because of your love.**
EPHESIANS 4:2 NLT

**If I know what love is, it is because of you.**

*Hermann Hesse*

XOXOXOXOXOXOXOXOXOXO

DATE __/__/__

*I thank God that He has caused me to forget my past pains because of my present pleasures.*

*My prayer is that He continues to bless you with the same.*

Joseph named the firstborn
Manasseh (Forget), saying,
"God made me forget all my hardships
and my parental home."
GENESIS 41:51 THE MESSAGE

When you hold on to your history you
do it at the expense of your destiny.

*T. D. Jakes*

DATE __/__/__

*I pray that God blesses you with many smiles and an unshakable Twinkle in your eyes.*

A twinkle in the eye means
joy in the heart,
and good news makes you feel
fit as a fiddle.
PROVERBS 15:30 THE MESSAGE

When I saw you, I fell in love,
and you smiled because you knew.

*William Shakespeare*

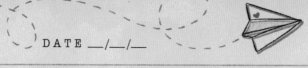

DATE __/__/__

*I know it can be hard to wait on something. So I ask God to strengthen your heart. I know you'll get through this. I love you.*

The LORD longs to be gracious to you;
therefore He will rise up to
show you compassion.
For the LORD is a God of justice.
Blessed are all who wait for Him!

ISAIAH 30:18 NIV

Compassion in a marriage relationship
often comes clothed in quiet. A hand held.
A tear wiped. Or even a tear shared. It's
found in giving space when space is needed.
Prayer when words won't work.

HEATHER HAIR

*I asked God to help you feel really, really loved and appreciated too. (Do you?)*

You turned my wailing into dancing;
You removed my sackcloth
and clothed me with joy.

PSALM 30:11 NIV

There is no charm equal
to tenderness of heart.

*Jane Austen*

DATE __/__/__

*I ask God to let you feel
His loving arms today.
He adores you.
Believe it.*

The LORD himself goes before you
and will be with you; He will never
leave you nor forsake you.
Do not be afraid; do not be discouraged.
DEUTERONOMY 31:8 NIV

To fall in love with God is the greatest
romance; to seek Him, the greatest
adventure; to find Him, the greatest
human achievement.

*St. Augustine*

DATE __/__/__

*I pray that*
*God lets you experience rest—and gives*
*you wisdom about how to create more*
*margin for yourself. I know life gets busy,*
*but taking a break is healthy and wise.*

I said, "Oh, that I had the wings of a dove!
I would fly away and be at rest."
PSALM 55:6 NIV

Rest time is not waste time. It is economy
to gather fresh strength.... It is wisdom
to take occasional furlough. In the long run,
we shall do more by sometimes doing less.

*Charles Spurgeon*

XOXOXOXOXOXOXOXOXO

DATE __/__/__

I asked God to help you spot an extra-special blessing from Him this week. Let me know when He does. I can't wait to celebrate with you.

**Every good and perfect gift is from above, coming down from the Father of the heavenly lights, who does not change like shifting shadows.**
JAMES 1:17 NIV

**Confidently receive God's abundant blessings. Think abundance, prosperity, and the best of everything.**

Norman Vincent Peale

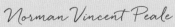

*I love that I can
be totally myself with you.
And that you can be you. I pray
God blesses us with the freedom
to always be transparent
and genuine around each other.*

The LORD does not look at the things people
look at. People look at the outward appearance,
but the LORD looks at the heart.

I SAMUEL 16:7 NIV

We need people who can see our faces without
makeup and our souls without scripts and our
lives without the polish and practice.

*Holley Gerth*

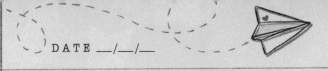

DATE __/__/__

*I pray that God encourages our children to pursue a godly marriage and be guided by what they have witnessed in us.*

**All your children will be
taught by the Lord,
and great will be their peace.**
ISAIAH 54:13 NIV

I want the kind of marriage that
makes my kids want to get married.
EMILY WIERENGA

I am grateful that God is my Source of all that I need. But I am also grateful He gave me a close second in you. I need you like a heart needs a beat.

I slept but my heart was awake.

SONG OF SONGS 5:2 NIV

Of all the music that reached farthest into heaven, it is the beating of a loving heart.

*Henry Ward Beecher*

*I want you to have this small gift, filled with big love. I pray it brightens your day.*

**She brings him good, not harm,
all the days of her life.**
PROVERBS 31:12 NIV

**He who loves with purity considers
not the gift of the lover,
but the love of the giver.**

*Thomas à Kempis*

DATE ___/___/___

*I pray that God gives you strength—His strength— when you need it most.*

**I can do all things through Him who strengthens me.**
PHILIPPIANS 4:13 NASB

**His strength is perfect when our strength is gone. He'll carry us when we can't carry on. Raised in His power, the weak become strong. His strength is perfect.**

*Steven Curtis Chapman*

X O X O X O X O X O X O X O X O X O

DATE __/__/__

*God wants you to do something very, very big for Him. He's just waiting on the perfect time. I pray He gives you patience as you wait.*

The vision is yet for the appointed time;
it hastens toward the goal and it will not fail.
Though it tarries, wait for it;
for it will certainly come, it will not delay.

HABAKKUK 2:3 NASB

Teach us, O Lord, the disciplines
of patience, for to wait
is often harder than to work.

*Peter Marshall*

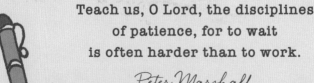

*I pray God draws
us deeper into an intimate
relationship, not only
with Him but with
each other as well.*

Let Him lead me to the banquet hall,
and let His banner over me be love.
SONG OF SOLOMON 2:4 NIV

The only true language
in the world is a kiss.

*Alfred de Musset*

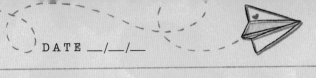

I will love you until the stars
go out and the tides no longer ebb
and flow. God will too.
I pray you bask in that love today...
and always.

**I have loved you with an
everlasting love;
therefore I have drawn you
with lovingkindness.**
JEREMIAH 31:3 NASB

To love abundantly is to live
abundantly, and to love forever
is to live forever.
HENRY DRUMMOND

*I pray that God blesses you with the warmth of my love every moment you are away.*

"The LORD bless you and keep you."

NUMBERS 6:24 NIV

Love wholeheartedly, be surprised, give thanks and praise. Then you will discover the fullness of your life.

*David Steindl-Rast*

*I pray that God fills you to the brim with joy and then tops it off until it overflows.*

O taste and see that the LORD is good.

PSALM 34:8 NASB

Love is the master key that opens the gates of happiness.

*Oliver Wendell Holmes*

DATE __/__/__

*I thank God for our ordinary moments in our ordinary days. Savoring the ordinary can mean simple satisfaction with life and each other.*

The Lord takes delight in His people;
He crowns the humble with victory.

PSALM 149:4 NIV

Love doesn't make the world go round.
Love is what makes the ride worthwhile.

*Franklin P. Jones*

OXOXOXOXOXOXOXOXO

DATE __/__/__

*I ask God to bless us by increasing the level of our experience of Him in our marriage.*

**The blessing of the LORD brings wealth, without painful toil for it.**

PROVERBS 10:22 NIV

Simply put, God favors those who ask. He holds back nothing from those who want and earnestly long for what He wants.

*Bruce Wilkinson*

DATE __/__/__

*Any idea how truly talented, strong, and valuable you are? In case you forgot, I asked God to remind you just how much today. (Imagine arms stretched as wide as New York to Los Angeles!) Yeah, that much.*

Encourage one another and build each other up, just as in fact you are doing.
I THESSALONIANS 5:11 NIV

Of all of the places on the planet,
your marriage should be that one place
where you are encouraged, reminded of your
strengths, and given the motivation
you need to live out those strengths well.

*Tony Evans*

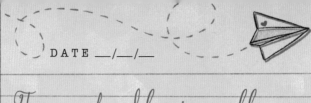

DATE __/__/__

I pray for blessings all over
our marriage—blessings
like peace, kindness, purpose,
and hope. I know God is
answering my prayer.
Get ready for snuggle season.

**The LORD turn His face toward
you and give you peace.**
NUMBERS 6:26 NIV

Blessed are the single-hearted,
for they shall enjoy much peace.
AMY CARMICHAEL

DaySpring

*I thanked God today:*
*He chose wisely*
*in giving you to me.*

The LORD God said, "It is not good
for the man to be alone. I will make
a helper suitable for him."

GENESIS 2:18 NIV

I would not wish any companion
in the world but you.

*William Shakespeare*

DaySpring

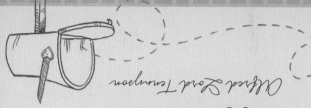

If I had a flower for every time I thought of you...I could walk through my garden forever."

*Alfred Lord Tennyson*

**Pray continually.**

1 THESSALONIANS 5:17 NIV

Thinking of you makes my day. Talking to God about you makes my life. Praying for you is my greatest joy.